For...

*Albert Einstein who posts the most
vital question on behalf of humanity...*

And For...

*The Buddha who gives the precise
answer to mankind.*

Einstein Questions, Buddha Answers

First Edition : May, 2005

price : 180 Baht

National Library of Thailand Cataloging in Publication Data

Supawan P. Panawong Green

Einstein Questions, Buddha Answers.---Pathumthani :
Skybook, 2005.

Pages No. 112

1. Buddhism and Science   2. Dharma (Buddhism)

I. Tittle.

294.31175

ISBN 974-93091-4-6

Distributed by :

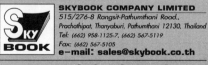

SKYBOOK COMPANY LIMITED
515/276-8 Rangsit-Pathumthani Road.,
Prachathipat, Thanyaburi, Pathumthani 12130, Thailand
Tel: (662) 958-1125-7, (662) 567-5119
Fax: (662) 567-5105
e−mail: sales@skybook.co.th

www.skybook.co.th

Printed at : Kilen Company Limited
Tel : (662) 0-2694-3010

Contents

Einstein Questions, Buddha Answers

Introduction

When I began writing the introduction for *Do You Know What A Normal Mind Is?*, it was two weeks after the devastating tsunami hit Asia. I got carried away; the text was too long and I couldn't use it. Instead of discarding them into my recycle bin, I turned them into this little book you are reading right now.

This booklet is a good introduction inviting you to explore the rest of my written works, some of which have been published and some are posted in my website.

The heart of my work is about letting people know there is *'the ultimate truth'* as well as guiding people to have access to it.

The title of this book is my intention to bridge the gap between science and religion and bring humanity to meet at the central platform of truth, modesty, simplicity and humility. By using my non-religious approach, it is very much possible that individuals of all races, nations and beliefs are able to glimpse the ultimate truth provided that they could be open-minded, remain neutral and read my works without any pre-judgement.

The definition of 'truth' is a 'fact' that has been verified. The shocking truth is that we are living in a society in which fact or truth can be spun; fabricated and turned into misinformation, half-truth, complete lies and propaganda. Verification can easily turn into an alibi instead. Not to mention countries with despotism, whose people don't know truth form lies. Even nations under the huge umbrella of outstanding democracy, her people are often left feeling confused, not knowing what the 'truth' is - whatever truth is concerned.

In our contemporary affluent society, truth relates closely with mega wealth and political power. It depends on who owns the media, the press as well as the artistic work of PR, advertising and particularly 'spin doctors' whose jobs are to reshape facts into whatever they want the facts to turn out. 'Keeping up appearances' is much more important than the whole chunk of truth, which may often be ugly. The lack of honesty and integrity among the rich and the powerful are parts of the main reasons that throw the world society into chaos and inflict unnecessary suffering to humankind.

Consequently, some of our history could well be a pack of lies; we don't know for sure if man ever set foot on the moon; who killed JFK; who were behind 9/11; what about the weapon of mass destructions that was supposed to be the main reason to justify the war with Iraq, the Holy Grail was a holy cup or holy blood, the list of conspiracy can go on forever. I am sure some of you must know much more than I do.

At least, we know the Asian tsunami was the criminal responsible for the death and the suffering of millions of people on Boxing Day, 2004, but as far as the long list of man-made human tragedies is concerned, we may never know who the real perpetrators are!

Without knowing the ultimate truth, we can only settle our scores and differences with relative truth - spun truth, half-truth or propaganda! How can bits and pieces of truth solve any problem at all? Could the absence of the whole truth be the root cause of all our conflicts and clashes, which prevent mankind from living together in harmony?

If it does, it is very important for us to keep pulling on the string of truth, to get to the end of it or till we can reach the nature of the ultimate truth. Only then, could we know truth from lies. This task certainly requires a great deal of very careful investigation and guided wisdom, which all my written works can hopefully assist you with the perspective.

Apart from trying to help you to understand the truth on the thinking level, I also want to help you to initiate your journey of finding the truth, which cannot be accomplished by reading alone. You must engage in training certain mental skill, which is the Buddhist meditation practice called vipassana or the four foundations of mindfulness. My teaching at the University of Birmingham purely focuses on initiating and developing this vital mental skill for students in a non-religious approach by using Tai chi qi gong movements.

This works out very well because it combines the care of physical, mental and spiritual health all in one practice.

Attempting to raise awareness for my books so that my message can reach the wider audience, my friends and supporters in Thailand have urged me to kindly ask either His Holiness, The Dalai Lama or the most venerable Tish Nat Han to write a foreword for *Do You Know What A Normal Mind Is?*

Despite the huge piece of message I've been passing on to my fellow human friends for some years, I, somehow, feel extremely normal and ordinary in my heart. Being a housewife, I had never thought that my works were the material for the Dalai Lama, whom I place on the very high moral and spiritual platform, until the moment I read my friend's email.

I told my family about my friends' advice and we joyfully talked about the humorous side of this story. Then my youngest son came up with further idea that I should also write to famous Buddhists and ask for one or two sentences of feedback for me to use as the blurb for my back cover as he believed this would certainly draw people's attention. Colin was very enthusiastic, he helped me search the Internet and got hold of a list of Buddhist celebrities: Richard Gere, Orlando Bloom; Goldie Hawn; Susan Sarandon; Keanu Reeves. But for some unknown reason, I felt compelled to write to Michael Pailin who is not a Buddhist and has no belief in the rebirth. Colin also helped me compose letters ready to be sent off to celebrities when my manuscripts are ready.

By the time I finished writing the introduction and finalise the editing of that book, which was only couple weeks ago, a series of thoughts entered my head telling me to abandon the whole idea of writing to celebrities and even the Dalai Lama. Apart from the reason that my letters and manuscripts might have to sit on the desks of their agents for sometime, there is no guarantee they would have time to read my works, there are other reasons too.

The most important one is because my entire work is based on telling people that I know the ultimate truth. Should I truly have such wisdom, that knowledge alone should be able to carry me all the way through to the central stage. It is imperative I make a stand with my own words without extra help from famous people who may or may not know the ultimate truth themselves. This is something I must do to win your trust in my wisdom and your confidence in me as your guide. I think I owe you that much.

This is one way to help you to judge the quality of my knowledge and myself. I have said all along that the ultimate truth is nothing more than the state of sheer simplicity and ordinariness. The owners of real wisdom would certainly feel normal and truly grounded. It can be compared to a strong man lifting heavy weights without feeling the strain. What I have committed myself to is an enormous responsibility for a woman of my status. How can I possibly lift this giant weight without real strength?

Now that I have no problem with myself and I am fortunate enough to have the ability to share this precious gift with you, I cannot see reasons why I should not help you. With the little time I have left in this world, I naturally feel that I must do my very best to pluck a few more lives out of this whirlpool of misery and guide them towards the 'Exodus Trail.' This is how I can still sit here and pen all these challenging words to papers.

I also want to prove to you that I don't set out to sell my books to make lots of money or to find fame. When I started writing my first book some 12 years ago, I have told myself that if only my book could help just one person on earth, it was worth my effort already. Although a number of readers already wrote and told me that they were that 'one person', my aim remains the same even today. Helping just one person at a time is the only way I know how to do my work as far as propagating the ultimate truth is concerned.

Therefore, if my books never stand a chance in the world market, so be it! That doesn't worry me in a slightest. I don't see it as a problem on my part at all. Should my books, however, miraculously become a hit - not in a million years! - it still wouldn't be for my benefit, the advantage is entirely yours, the reader. It means that I might have more people writing to me saying: *'I am that "one person" you plucked out from the whirlpool of misery, thank you.'* The most I do is smile and be happy for you: knowing that one more person has bought himself/herself the one way ticket and joined the 'Exodus Trail,' leaving the longest ring road of sorrow behind for good.

I have been through enough obstacles in the past 16 years, ever since I decided to teach meditation in my Tai chi class at the University of Birmingham. I have had to fight through both the inner and external battlefields to make sure that you would hear of this good news from me. Those painful encounters were very private and not at all easy to express especially with my handicapped English. I have, however, come a long way since. I now have a small group of devoted people helping me in Thailand: creating and looking after a website for me, raising fund to print my books, organising the forthcoming retreat and so on. These are the luxuries I never had before and I will make sure I don't take them for granted. The good sale of my books is, therefore, the very least of my concern.

I also look at this issue - not involving famous people for their comments - as a good challenge on your part as the readers. Are you going to read my books and agree with what I said only because celebrities gave me good comments, or you agree with me because my words alone are enough to inspire you to search for your true-self. This is the very first lesson I offer you now should you want to know the ultimate truth. You might as well get used to making your own judgements without asking others because you will have to make many more from now on. The path to the truth is a very lonely one and it is best if you can be independent. This is exactly what I have to do and to be, which make me qualify to talk to you so bluntly like this.

After the publications of my 4 Thai books, there are mix responses from Thai readers, ranging from the extreme optimists to the extreme negative remarks, which are to be expected. Writers, who agree to have their literary works published, must be well prepared for all kinds of reactions, positive and negative alike; it is impossible to please everyone. It is even more so with my area of knowledge, which has high level of sensitivity and controversy, it bounds to invite challenge, if not fierce attack. The downbeat comments usually say I am a 'self deluded' person. Only a few weeks ago, after reading my newly published book, a reader and a lawyer told his friend who is also my friend: *'your friend should have her head checked out by a shrink!'*[1] Yes, running to a professional is what we are so keen to do, aren't we? Who then would be qualified to check out the head of a psychiatrist?! Have you ever questioned?

Human are individuals, no two persons alike even identical twins; we have different character and personality, diverse level of mentality and spiritual potential, which make every person unique and interesting in his/her own way. Nonetheless, the Buddha says: wise people in this world are as many as the number of a cow's horns whereas ignorant people are as many as the number of hairs on a cow's body. Now, you can understand why I vow to help just 'one person' at a time, can't you?

---

[1] Please read chapter one: *A boost to Your Confidence* of the unfinished book *The User Guide to Life: Hello Tom Goodbye Jerry* in my website www. supawangreen.in.th

I could have concealed such disparaging remark from you, the English-speaking readers but I don't want to because I think this kind of downbeat is a good challenge for you. Are you going to be doubtful and put off by such critical comments? Or are you going to be your own person and be the judge for yourself? This is something you must work out by yourself. No one can really help you. This is why the contents of my work are made up of a bit of my knowledge and a bit of myself. I do this on purpose so that you have ways to assess myself without asking others.

Having said all those, some readers may think my speeches are rather contradicting because according to my letter written on 17 Feb. 2004, I did ask my students and readers for help. Please understand that asking (famous) people to endorse my ultimate knowledge is very much different from asking people to help spreading my knowledge to the wider audience. You may help me with the latter by all means but not the former unless your knowledge is compatible to those of mine or above. The mentioned letter is at the end of this book.

As far as the feedback is concerned, I must not overlook those of my students who have trained directly with me; some of them have become my dear friends like Juliet Banyard and Jianhui Xiong whom I have regular contacts.[2] The responses, I have had, range from students, career people, to working class people and housewife, all of whom came from different religious backgrounds: Catholic, Anglican, Sikh, Islam, Buddhist, atheist and agnostic. As far as I am concerned, their responses are as effective, if not, better than of those who knew me from my books only. The feedback from those who knew me personally can certainly eliminate hypocrisy from my written work. In this day and age, we know far too well that words can be one thing but personal life can be another. The heart of my work is to bring back our lost simplicity and ordinariness in people from all walks of life. Simplicity indeed is what I am and that's all there is to be known. Only people who have known me personally can give you the right message about myself. I have posted a file of feedback and

---

[2]Juliet wrote the foreword for *The User Guide to Life.*

some of my personal correspondence in my website for you to browse through.

You may ask: how about the profit I would make from the sale of my books. Well, they will be put straight back into the printing fund to print the next book on the list. Apart from the information I gave you at the end of this booklet: *How to help Supawan*, I have already explained to my Thai readers that when the printing fund is healthy enough in the future, I would have to accept 'a salary' by taking a fixed percentage from the fund. The simple reason is because I still have responsibility and commitment with my own family both here in Britain and in Thailand. My literary workloads have restricted me from getting a full time job all these years. Although my husband could do with my taking more financial responsibility, he kindly let me pursue my passion in writing and my few hours a week teaching at the University. Even my few hours of earning a small sum of money have been affected by a combination of reasons: my poor teaching, poor management, social change (could have something to do with the mobile phone generation) or simply because the hairs on a cow's body out number the horns! Consequently, my teaching hours per week has dwindled, from 7 hours/classes for 10 years down to 6 hours/classes five years ago and down to 4 hours/classes this present spring term due to the low intakes. My teaching hours could be reduced again to just 2 classes next term. In fact, I don't mind at all; it means I have more time for my increasing writing workloads without being disrupted by the journey to work. My husband is, therefore, the sole breadwinner and we live on a very low-income budget all through our married life.

For those reasons, I have no shame to ask for financial help should I still want to carry on guiding you to join the Exodus Trail. By accepting a fixed salary from my printing fund, just like any working people, either monthly or annually is, in my opinion, the fairest solution. The one thing I vow not do is to accept cash directly from people (not including my own family and extremely closed friends) especially from the rich, the famous and the powerful - said first, just in case I might bump into some in the future! Although I trust my heart enough in not to do the wrong thing, I still want to protect myself further from being used as we all know money is man's worst enemy. I cannot afford to have any hidden agenda should I want to help you to know the truth. Hence it is best to come clean with you and to draw a clear line now, when there is not much money in my printing fund so that we all know where we stand.

Should you wish to help me propagate the ultimate truth, please pledge towards my printing fund, your pledge will directly support my livelihood too. My salary issue will be discussed among my supporters in due course and will be announced in my website.

Finally, the purpose of this book is also to let you know of my forthcoming retreat, which will take place in Thailand in July 2005. Should you be interested to join this retreat, the details are at the end of this book.

I hope I have explained myself well enough and enable you to enjoy reading this book as well as to explore further the heart of my work.

Supawan P.Panawong Green
19 February 2005
Birmingham,
Britain

What Is
A Normal Way Of Life?

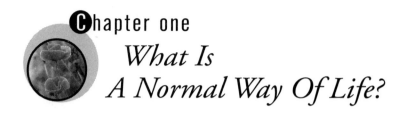

Chapter one
What Is
A Normal Way Of Life?

*I*t is very interesting to know what exactly is classed as normality or a normal way of life in today world shrouded by all kinds of problems caused by man and nature alike. Should you think normality is a subjective issue, this makes it even more important to know what normality really is or rather what a normal mind is. In the same way that 'world peace' has to be the accumulation of the individuals' peace put together, 'normality' or 'a normal way of life' of a collective society has to be the outcome of the normal minds of all individuals put together. Are they not?

Certain behaviours and actions that are perfectly normal to some people may be totally abnormal to another group of people. The same works in the opposite. It is perfectly normal for Western people to point things with their feet, but the same is classed as extremely rude and not normal for the Thai. Queuing is a very natural and normal social behaviour in Western society, but not to some Eastern and African countries!

A generation of bankrupts

It is true that every culture have its own set of values, norms, rules, laws and orders to be used as the standard assessing the level of normality, which obviously has everything to do with time and place.

Twenty-five years ago, I thought it was bad enough to go into debt to buy a house and went through countless of sleepless nights constantly worrying about our millstone. Whereas my children's generation find it rather normal to go into debts just to buy high tech gadgets, designer clothes and expensive beauty products, which, are often cast away once the novelty have worn out, and off they go chasing after yet another thrill that greedy merchants have lined up for them in our highly materialistic society. The whole philosophy of saving hard for something we really want has gone and replaced with, *I want it now.* With the extra help from the covetous irresponsible money-lenders who offer easy credits to young people without any control (from the government), this lethal combination has caused a generation of bankrupts.

It has been reported that people under 30 years of age are accounted for 60% of insolvencies in Britain.[3] This 'supposed to be normal' social value of this time and place is blatantly destructive: causing misery and breaking up families. It can easily lead to social chaos and meltdown. Under normal circumstances, life gets more difficult as we grow older: after being married with 2.4 children, there are more commitments and of course more necessary liabilities: mortgage, household bills, etc. Therefore, what kind of future our young generation is going to have?

The solution scales down to whether or not the government can come up with a set of 'right value' for our children. How can we educate our youngsters and

---

[3]Daily Mail Monday February 14, 2005

make sure they can stick to that set of 'right value'? To make it work, the government also has to make sure that greedy merchants do not exploit our youngsters' ignorance towards the reality of money lending. Stop glorifying debt by controlling the advertising business is a good start! Before the government can do any of those, she must, first of all, know what the 'right value' really is? Without this wisdom, there is no real solution.

When punishment involved

As the level of normality fluctuates through time and place and change from culture to culture, problems occur when punishment is involved. In the court of law in the democratic world, when the two opposing councils argue about right and wrong, just and unjust, fair and unfair, they are, in fact, arguing about believing in the different level of normality. One of the good examples is about the British farmer; Tony Martin was sentenced to three years imprisonment because he shot dead a burglar. Had he lived in the state of Texas, USA, he would have been rewarded with a healthy sum of money for killing the burglar instead of being thrown into jail. A matter like this is serious especially in the country where capital punishment is in forced. It needs the input of some real wisdom: requiring the knowledge of true normality to enable one to justify such a case.

Delusional triumph?

Some of us may think the issues of right and wrong, normal and abnormal are subjected to individuals' interpretations, therefore subjective. Some behaviours and actions may seem right and normal to some people but they are blatantly wrong and abnormal to others like this following example.

Recently, a 59-year-old British woman has just had her second IVF baby. She already has two grown up children in their 30s and has already been a grandmother. Her first IVF child is just two years old. The way she expressed herself as why she needed to have more children at this advanced age, sounded very normal - to her of course! In her own word, she was looking for an unconditional love that only a child can give her. If you think being a mother of two very young children at the age of 59 is bad enough, maybe you haven't heard of yet another woman of Romanian origin, gave birth to her baby girl at the age of 66 just two weeks after the British woman. Both women had undergone the fertility treatment for a number of years and had their babies through IVF.

Some may argue that these cases are not about right and wrong, normal or abnormal but about those two women's choices and their rights, which they are entitled to. There are, in fact, a number of better choices those two elderly women could have chosen - something that is a bit more normal like growing old gracefully! When individuals' seemingly wrong decisions affect the welfare of others especially children, we need to seriously straight things out; this has everything to do with the heart of my work. These historic cases are not just about two emotionally mixed up elderly women who had made some really wrong decisions, but this involves a whole team of medical professions and experts who are responsible for the IVF experiment, and whose knowledge and expertise allow such unnatural event to happen.

In the past, we did not have the scientific know-how to cheat the law of nature in this way. Women at that advanced age would gracefully settle down; most of them would be a grandmother or great grandmother and very content with their extended families. As for those, who could not have children, would have long dealt with their painful emotions due to the unfortunate circumstances, which, admittedly is part of life. But now, in the brave new world of the scientific achievement and the IVF industry, we seem to think that we have the rights to cheat the law of nature: human embryos can be frozen, motherhood can be put on hold, allowing women to pursue their professional career until the last possible moment, twins can be born a few years apart so that mothers don't have to work too hard and so on.

Would you really accept all these contemporary social phenomena as normality? Can these really be classed as human having control over nature? The doctors who treated those two elderly mothers seemed to think so. To them, this is the huge success as far as their professionalism is concerned. This is the scientific accomplishment they are very much proud of - having the ability to make post menopausal women become pregnant and carry the baby all the way till giving birth. But please think carefully as who pay the real price for this delusional triumph? Are they not the children and society? *'Should this kind of practice become more acceptable in the future, how long before we witness a surge in 'IVF orphans' whose elderly parents have not lived long enough to see them into adulthood and self-sufficiency?'*[4] Think...we must!

I have nothing against scientific researches and discoveries. The IVF experiment has already helped many childless couples to fulfil their strong instinct of parenthood. We already have a whole generation of IVF children well into their adulthoods. The discovery of DNA is also of immense importance.

---

[4]Daily Mail January 2005

Rowing a boat in a gigantic lake

What I am against is how those achievements are being used and what they are used for. When our intellectual knowledge is being used to exploit, to add misery, to harm and to kill people, we must seriously question the purpose of our knowledge. Without the clear purpose, our academic is inevitably misused for the sake of finding more wealth, fulfilling one's false dream, finding fame or just for the sake of gaining more knowledge - uncovering the unknown like the doctors who treated the above two women along with many more confidential researches done behind the closed door, which could cause the annihilation of the human race.

The greedy merchants who are responsible for the collapse of our younger generation could not have possibly made staggering amount of money should they not be intellectually clever. *Most of the ideas we hold today about how our economy does or should work stem from Adam Smith's 'The Wealth of Nations.'*

America was built on these principles and many Americans, both economists and citizens, still believe that Adam Smith's economic theory is the most accurate view of how the world actually works.[5] I quote this from the Internet because they could say much better than I can. Could this economic philosophy be the reason for our global wealth falling into the hands of a few mega rich merchants? Could this notion be responsible for the rich to get richer and the poor to get poorer and divide this 'third rock from the sun' into the first, the second and *'the third world country'*?

Without the clear perspective for our education, the nature of our pounding for more intellectual knowledge is merely a matter of rowing a boat in a gigantic lake: promoting health, longevity, technology and wealth, that's all there is to it. We feel that we have come a long way away from our ignorant ancestors but, in fact, we have reached nowhere whatsoever. We are going round the bend; we have no idea if we are moving forward or backward, towards left, right or

---

[5]www.heartoscotland.com Adam Smith Economist

centre. We are drowning in our mountain of intellectual knowledge. That's why the world is in this mess.

I listened to Tony Blair last night.[6] He admitted himself: *'...as you are trying to solve one problem, you are facing yet another problem along the line. Therefore you have to...'* Basically the British prime minister was describing the complexity of our society, where every problem is entangled like a huge ball of knotted cotton. No single problem is straight forward and easily thrashed out with one solution.

It doesn't matter who come into power, Labour, Tory, Republican or Democrat, our life span is not long enough to see that none of our political leaders can deliver what they have promised. It is impossible to get everything right because life is an on-going process; there are always new problems popping up. Please look back into the history of mankind; the world has always been troublesome with different nature of problems one way or another. What we don't know is, this is what life in prison is all about. You can't expect an easy ride

---

[6]Talk to the Prime Minister, channel five 16 February 2005

like living at home, can you? This is the wisdom that humanity is very much lack of and I am doing my best to offer to you.

The whole point is that as long as our leaders still don't have a clue what life is all about, there is no real solution to any problem at all. What we are doing right now is merely rearranging furniture into different location in the room, just to make the room looks new to our eyes, that's all there is to it. We haven't yet come out from our dark room, absolutely not.

Summary

The real purpose for our education is to take humanity out of this enormous prison cell of life. The nature of the ultimate truth must be clearly addressed. This wisdom is the beginning or the end of my figurative entangled cotton ball. Once this first domino is found; every problem will collapse accordingly. Only then will we know exactly what a normal way of life is. To pass on this message to humanity is the only priority; everything else is secondary.

Absolute Power

Corrupts Absolutely

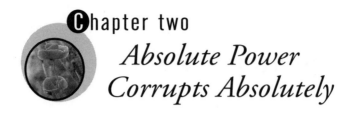

Chapter two
Absolute Power Corrupts Absolutely

Rulers' minds and the consequences

Let's investigate further, is it not the mind, which initially dictate our speech and actions? We do what our minds tell us to do, don't we? We say things that our minds tell us to say. If our minds are normal, our speeches, our decisions and our actions are subsequently normal, right? And this works the same in the opposite direction too. If our minds are not normal, neither will be our speech and actions.

We can, then, easily understand why the speech and decision making of our rulers are of utmost important because these people make the rules for the rest of us to abide by. If the states of mind of our rulers are not normal and not at peace, this would inevitably affect their way of thinking and so would their decision-makings. The final outcomes, political decisions leading to actions, would definitely affect all and everyone of us, the ruled. Consequently, our whole way of life, whether we would live in harmony, misery, suffering, anarchy, chaos, fear, etc, depends entirely on our rulers' state of minds. Are they not?

I am sure you have heard of this saying, *'Absolute power corrupts absolutely.'* Well, whoever said that must know how human's minds work. Simply having 'power' of any shape, form and level - not to mention having the absolute political power! - can easily corrupt, twist and push people's mind off the acceptable balance.

With that little bit of extra power!

Looking around our workplaces, we often see that a minor promotion with slightly higher position with that 'little bit of extra power', can easily change people's behaviour - just like that!

What do you think domestic violence and rape are? Apart from the issue of control, they are the exercise of men's power over women, as men exceed women in terms of physical strength.

When that little bit of extra power are in the hands of people who have conflicts or at war and are armed with weapons, the outcome can be catastrophic. As I am writing this paragraph, I am also looking at the front page of today paper with the graphic photographs showing Iraqi prisoners being abused by a few American and British soldiers. These pictures may seem shocking and appalling as the British prime minister has put it, but this abuse of power is no different from what the Iraqis did to the western soldiers when they were captured including the suicide bomb attack, the hostage abductions and their executions.

I am not comparing notes here as who could inflict more gruesome acts than who and to whom. Neither am I defending anyone or attempting to justify such appalling physical abuse on defenceless people, but let us not forget that Iraq was and still is a war zone - not Disney world! Human tragedies of all nature: killing, torturing, raping and so on, do happen in any battle zone, not just in Iraq.

Saving Private Ryan

As far as I am concerned, war is the ultimate nature of abnormality, of madness and sheer insanity. I am sure we've seen enough war films to know the horror of wars and the profound mental damages left behind. I like the theme in 'Saving Private Ryan'. In the midst of the complete madness of World War 2 where nothing made sense, setting a clear goal of plucking one man out of the mayhem and safely returning him to his mother, was an excellent idea - although still making no sense! At least, that temporary purpose could bring some sense back to the lives of those few soldiers. We all need to feel purposeful, worthy and have that sense of achievement even in normal circumstances, even more so in wartime. This film was also very good in depicting the graphic horror of war and hostilities. It should make us stay clear from war, but it doesn't seem to work at all, does it?

A war zone can be liken to a bowl of spaghettis tossed together with a series of hot spices: confusion, hatred, anger, vengeance, killing, torturing, raping, fear, pain, suffering and so on. Battlefields are hell, where every shred of internal and external normality is ripped, chopped and pound into mere dust, having no real meaning, let alone feeling it.

Even in a supposedly 'normal society' surrounded by a supposedly 'normal way of life' - whatever that is! - people still find it difficult to have good grip over their minds when they have to face challenging situations. Therefore, in the war-stricken countries, it is understandable that people's minds are many times more at risk of being pushed off balance than those who are fortunate enough to live in peaceful countries. The mentioned ugly events above are not at all unexpected.

If anyone should be condemned at all, they are the government leaders of all parties who started this war or any war at the first place. Then again, the reasons to start a war have never been straightforward matters, have they?

Nevertheless, this misuse of power is also no different to those cruel and ugly activities done behind the closed doors, away from the cameras. Mistreating prisoners of conscience or any prisoners is almost the routine practice for undemocratic governments and surprisingly in some democratic countries too. I am sure Amnesty International can come up with some very handy information regarding Human Rights of democratic and undemocratic governments alike.

Unless you are a saint

There is a Thai saying: *'Stay away from mad and drunken people.'* I didn't quite understand why until recent years when I finally understand how human minds work and what a normal mind is. The reason behind that saying is that mad and drunken people are very strong minded, and if anyone with softer minds stays too close to them, they can convince you to believe in anything at all: being a dog can be better than being a man!

To identify a normal mind is not easy because mental damage is not as obvious as physical wounds. Therefore, you must, first of all, know what a normal mind is. In other words, you must know what the ultimate truth is. Only then can you distinguish a good and normal mind from a twisted and damaged mind.

A tyrant's mind must be millions time stronger than a mere mad or a drunken mind due to the immense power one holds. Unless one is a real saint, possessing the absolute political power can definitely twist one's mind towards insanity and abnormality in no time at all. It isn't wrong to say that all tyrants' minds have different degree of insanity and abnormality in them - of course, unless you are a saint!

Free Tibet

A true saint with absolute political power would undoubtedly transform his immense power into goodness: for the peace, the happiness and the well-being of his people. It is a great pity that the Chinese government wouldn't allow the Dalai Lama to prove this theory! I really hope that the Dalai Lama could, one day, return home to Tibet with the full autonomy over his country and his people. I fully support all actions as far as freeing Tibet is concerned.

Hitler

With their absolute power at dispense, tyrants can make up their own set of rules: making wrong into right and right into wrong. With the immense strength of an insane mind, a charismatic dictator can convince and mobilise a big number of people to do exactly the things he wants them to do. Strong or not, Hitler successfully convinced the tens of thousands of the Nazis and the SS (thugs) to believe that the Jews were nothing more than subhuman and it was justify to wipe them out from the surface of the earth.

January 2005 is the 60th anniversary of the liberation of Auschwitz where one million and one thousand Jews were systematically killed. I have too much respect for humankind and cause me to believe that such inconceivable acts of the Nazis to the Jews could only be the result of a big bunch of utterly abnormal and twisted minds put together: of course, they themselves didn't know.

I have watched a few documentaries during this Auschwitz season. Several interviews from people who had first hand experiences repeat the same statements that the Nazis showed no remorse in the most horrendous crime they had committed. In fact, that was the right feeling to the Nazis. They must strongly believe that they were doing the right thing. Without such false and delusional conviction, the holocaust of the Jews could not possibly have happened.

Sane people with their normal minds could not possibly be misled by such delusional, devilish thoughts of their fellow human-beings and agree to join Hitler's criminal enterprise, to be used as his killing machine, resulting in mass systematic extermination of millions of the Jews.

Some holocaust critics said that Hitler couldn't have possibly wiped out the 6 millions Jews, not without the support of the German nation at the time. It may sound logical but I still feel reluctant to believe so, once again, I have too much respect for human race. My view may be too optimistic, if not downright naïve and may offend the holocaust victims. I, however, want to think there are kind, merciful and loving people in all races including the Germans even at wartime.

Let's not forget Oskar Schindler, a member of the Nazi party and war profiteer who rescued over 1000 Jews from the hands of the Nazis during the Holocaust. I know there is no match whatsoever between the numbers saved and the number killed, but to those 1000 lives, it meant everything to them. Another person worth mentioned here is Colonel Claus Von Stauffenberg, one of the Nazis top officials who led the secret plot to kill

Hitler in 1944, but his attempt failed and he was later executed.

The German nation should not feel offended over this constant digging of the Nazis and their notorious legacy - as I am doing now! - because this chapter of history is one of the most expensive lessons, humanity must learn and do our best to prevent. Such acts of sheer evil, however, were not just about Hitler, the Nazis or the SS. This is about the nature of an extremely twisted mind of a human being who happened to have absolute power in his hand. It could be anyone of any race; whoever has the grip of such absolute power and whenever it may happen, the result is always the same - all hells break lose!

Mao Tse Tung

As a matter of fact, Mao Tse Tung, my own race, killed many times more people than Hitler did. Not until I read *'Wild Swans'*, the story of three extraordinary women of China (written by Jung Chang 1992), did I fully realise the extent of horror the Chinese were inflicted upon under Mao's cruel regime. The consequence of Mao's Great Leap Forward 1958-1963 left an estimate 20 millions Chinese died of starvation or disease related to starvation; 9 millions alone were starved to death in 1960, not to mentioned the death tolls through executions of those branded 'anti-revolutionary' and hard labours in various rehabilitation camps throughout China. People were reduced to eat the cultured layer of their own urine. Apart from a handful elites, there wasn't a single ordinary family in China who didn't lose at least one member of their immediate families.

With his utterly twisted and insane mind, Mao didn't have a clue what he had put his people through. To Mao, 30 millions was just a few grain of salt comparing to a billion population, so what? As far as I am concerned, this overwhelming human catastrophe was the result of an insane mind, to begin with!

Pol Pot

So did Pol Pot and his malevolent act. When I look at the Cambodian people now, I cannot imagine that this Buddhist nation - whose people, the faithful followers of the Buddha, are supposedly believing in the law of karma, in the non-violence and in sharing the loving kindness to all sentient beings - could have engaged in such shameful and satanic acts.

In the case of Pol Pot, we must seriously learn that never put ultimate power, meaning weapons, in the hands of ordinary people. When Pol Pot came into power - by taking advantage of the confusion resulted from Vietnam war, causing the chaos in the whole of the South East Asia region - the Khmer Rouge (mainly uneducated peasants and ordinary Cambodian people, the previous under-privilege class of the old regime) who never had a taste of 'that extra bit of power' before, were suddenly put in charge, armed and had the ultimate power over the life and death of their fellow brothers and sisters. Of course, such immense power was far too much for ordinary human mind to handle, resulting in the genocide of the Cambodian people.

Such enormous power was more than enough to corrupt even a mind of a single moral human being - I am sure you heard of famous monks and member of the clergy who behaved badly - let alone the minds of a huge pact of uneducated people. This dangerous combination have become the most lethal ingredients that, beyond any doubt, would corrupt and twist people's minds to their extreme: dehumanise the supposedly kind and serene people into sheer instinctive animals; utterly shocking!

The Khmer Rouge under Pol Pot, the SS under Hitler were nothing more than a bunch of hooligans, thugs, yobs, morons who, before the war, hung around street corners and caused troubles anyway even without power in their hands. Every country has this type of people, even today, and they are responsible for street crimes of all sorts. It is due to their governments whether or not they know how to divert and turn all their pent-up energy into positive activities instead;

otherwise troubles of all nature are to be expected from this group of people.

An untrained mind cannot be trusted

Why it is so important to know what a normal mind is because our world history, may be in smaller scale, keeps on repeating these horrendous, satanic events even in this day and age: the former Yugoslavia, Croatia, Iraq, Rwanda, Sudan, Somalia, North Korea, Burma and all the countries ruled by tyrants before and right now. It proves that we haven't learnt much from our evil past: not at all remote, these entire human catastrophes happened in the living memories of our grandparents, parents and ourselves.

Nevertheless, all these inconceivable horrors inflicting on humanity can only confirm the wisdom of the Buddha: *'an untrained mind cannot be trusted.'* Human's minds that have never been polished by moral value and refined by certain meditation skill cannot be trusted. These untrained minds are easily misled and influenced by money, fame and power. Without meditation skill, guilty conscience is the only factor that can prevent people from wrong doing and can sustain a good balance of a human mind. Without moral conscience, a man is equal, if not, worse than animals.

Summary

Whether people turn out to be destructive citizen or good Samaritans depends entirely on the actions of the governments and their philosophy of education.

Once again, this has everything to do with whether or not we know the ultimate truth. Once the truth (the beginning or the end of an entangled ball of cotton) is properly addressed, training the minds of individuals towards the right direction will subsequently be possible. Consequently problems of all nature will be resolved accordingly.

Suffering Goes On

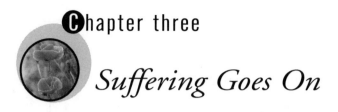

Chapter three

Suffering Goes On

*L*et's look at our supposedly 'normal society' with supposedly 'normal way of life' and see how normal we really are. It is easy to judge that tyrannical ruled society is not normal - if we are lucky enough to judge them from the free world. But does it mean that in just living in a democratic society, our set of rules can always be classed as normal?

Drinking culture, the extra help!

Let's have a look of the controversial Licensing Bill that currently capture the Press and the interest of the British public. To the standard of the British people, drinking is classed as normal acceptable behaviour. It isn't a surprise if there might be more pubs than churches in Britain: people seem to use pubs as signposts for guiding directions. Is it because of this normal behaviour that caused the present British Culture Secretary making it legal for pubs to be opened 24 hours a day?! This proposal would inevitably encourage excessive and binge drinking, the root cause of many other social problems to come: domestic violence, divorce, ill health, etc. Just in case if my readers outside the United Kingdom don't quite know the full extent of the problems. Here are some facts and figures.

'Already, alcohol-related diseases cost the British National Health Service about 1.7 billion every year. It has gone up ten fold since the 1970s. Also around 17 million working days are lost annually because of alcohol abuse, costing our economy £6.4 billion. More than half of the violent crime is related to drink.' (Daily Mail Wednesday, January 12, 2005)

Any government would be disturbed by these facts and figures. If this Licensing Bill along with the Gambling Law - allowing the Las Vegas type of gambling on British soil - are in forced, this would undoubtedly contribute towards the course of twisting people's minds even tighter and result in more social unrest. It means that two out of five fundamental moral precepts have been violated with the direct help from the government. Even without the extra help, society has already burdened a long series of problems, which directly affect the well-being of our daily lives: ranging from family breakdowns, unemployment, poverty, frauds of all sorts resulting from the computer and mobile phone technology, ill health, crimes of all natures to the constant threat of terrorism. These are already enough reasons to cause people feeling everything but normal.

The magnitude of human tragedies - affected by everyday difficulties big and small alike - put together over the years are overwhelmingly colossal, leaving a great number of people feeling most vulnerable and insecure one way or another. The rising suicide rate and the booming of both legal and illegal drugs industry in all society are good indications showing the high level of abnormality in the minds of the publics and the disarray in our civilisation.

All these tangled up problems cannot be straight out unless our education has the crucial knowledge about the nature of the truth or a normal mind and how to get to it.

Let's not forget we are mortal

Not only man, nature too can contribute towards our mental weakness, vulnerability and isolation. Unavoidable accidents, physical illnesses and death, although are parts of the deal of living, most people still find it hard to accept when these unfortunate events finally knock on our doors. When our loved ones or we are struck down by serious or terminal illnesses, fatal accidents or death, our hearts are crushed and our mental pains are excruciating; normality becomes meaningless.

We may think medical science is the answer as it can help us to have better health and prolong life. It may be true but after a few more years or even some 10 to 20 years of our extended lease of life, we still have to die, haven't we? Human is mortal, please don't forget. Our wake-up calls, reminding of our own death, are everywhere. We hear of people either already dead or dying all the time. But amazingly, most people can't seem to grasp the fact that they could be next.

The truth is as we are creeping into our old age, we may not want to admit to others but elderly people know far too well of those familiar, anxious and lonely feelings that keep on biting their lives away from the inside, and there is absolutely no one can help them. We are all alone as far as death is concerned. This is the exact reason why religious faith comes into the equation of life.

Tsunami disaster: the courtesy call!

There is no rule saying that old people must die first. Even young people, as we all know, can be threatened by sudden death too. The recent tsunami disaster, which hit 12 countries around the Indian Ocean and claimed more than 220,000 lives, was yet another courtesy calls from Heaven, God, Mother Nature or whatever you want to call. Sadly, a third of the tsunami victims were children who were too young and too innocent to know the danger and to withstand the awesome force of nature. This overwhelming devastation has reinforced our pitiless universe and the unpredictable overpowering force of nature that is capable to throw thousands of people to their death in an instant and leave millions living in immense suffering.

This mammoth human tragedy caused by the act of nature was far from a wake up call, it was merely yet another courteous call on top of many other calamities in the past, not at all remote: in 1965, an Indian drought wiped out 1.5 million people, in 1970, a Bangladesh cyclone left 500,000 dead, in 1976, an earthquake in China caused 242,800 fatalities.

Mental tsunami

Why this apocalyptic devastation affected the whole of our world community and manage to pledge the unprecedented amount of money is because there are 50 nations among the death toll of some 220,000 and we also witnessed this horrific events as if it was happening in our living rooms, which make this giant wave become real and hit us all.

This overwhelming human tragedy has subsequently caused yet another devastating mental tsunami hitting many more millions of people around the globe: submerging our inner lives beneath floods of painful emotions, gagging us for air.

Unlike the giant wave that came, receded and left - everything was done and dusted within 10-30 minutes depending on the area where the wave hit - our mental tsunami will never retreat from our minds; it will keep on drowning our inner lives for many years to come depending on the individual circumstance and how strong one's mind is to withstand one's mental pain.

Talking directly to tsunami victims

Since this book will mostly be read among the English speaking readers (westerners), therefore I will focus on this group of people by giving the relevant examples, you can relate to, and not because I don't care about the millions of the locals: the Indonesians, the Thais, The Malaysian, the Sri Lakans, the Indians, the Maldivian, the Somalian and so on.

The most hit group of people are the survived victims who have been through the horrifying ordeals with the giant waves and have lost their loved ones. Their physical wounds, if they had one, would soon heal, but not their mental damages as their mental-selves are still and will be under water for a long time: being drowned in floods of painful emotions and terrifying flashbacks. Some may lose the will of living especially those who have lost most of their immediate families, as they could not see how life could ever be normal again. Some were forced to make the unimaginable decisions during their ordeals and those decisions would stay with them for life.

What if...

One of the most poignant stories was an Australian mother who was in Phuket - if I remember correctly -

with her two boys, age between 7-10 years old. When the wave struck, she could not possibly hold on to both her boys and was forced to let go one of them so that she could save the other son. In that spur of the moment, she had to make this impossible and most painful choice - which no mother should be allowed to make - of letting go of her elder child. Even though her elder boy had survived in the end, such unimaginable choice would stay and haunt her for life. She will be hearing the words 'what if?' in her head for a long time, maybe for the rest of her life and so will millions of other tsunami victims who were in the same predicament like this mother.

There was another sad story of a young lady who was on holiday in that region, I am not sure of her nation of origin, British or American. The giant wave had pushed her under water and she was trapped under some big object, a man managed to pull her out, allowing her to emerge but she couldn't see the man who had helped her: believing that he might be drown. As she was holding on to the pole, another girl nearby reaching her hand out to her, obviously wanting to grab hold of her, but she knew she didn't have enough strength to do so. Had she done it, she might not have lived to tell this tale. She saw that girl emerging twice; as she went down the third time, she never came back up again.

Although everyone in the world would totally understand her agonizing predicament and decision, it won't make any slight difference to the way she has been feeling and only she knows the full extent of horror that are still playing in her mind.

Sadly, there are no shortage of such first hand experiences and stories about the 2004 Asian tsunami which would, beyond any doubt, leave both the direct and indirect victims, went through the opposite end of the emotional spectrum: from the extreme fear of losing their loved ones to the extreme happiness and huge relief of finding them alive; from the hope of finding the missing loved ones alive to the painful acceptance of confirming their deaths; some are still living in their emotional limbo, not allowed to grieve properly and still hang on to that faintest hope of finding their loved ones alive, as there are yet an estimate of a hundred thousands of humanity remain missing, a great number of those will never be found.

Everything but normal

Under normal circumstance, some people are mentally stronger than others and are able to deal with the toughness of situation accordingly. The Asian tsunami is everything but normal circumstance.

No matter how resilient some of us are; human's minds have their pain threshold. The repeated heart rending scenes of extreme human emotions at their most raw - panic people running away from the gigantic pounding wave, some were submerged, some were hanging on trees or buildings with their dear life, after the recede of the flood, corpses were everywhere; panic faces looking for their loved ones; shell shocked mothers and fathers found their dead children, wailing like being put through a slaughter house, some trying desperately to revive their babies, frantically looking for a button of life somewhere on their motionless bodies to switch back on, children screaming, sobbing their heart out and refusing to part from their dead parents, etc - were unbearable to watch from the television screen. Two British brothers holidaying in Sri Lanka at the time said, *'it was much easier to keep on digging the trench and bury the dead than facing the unthinkable grieve these people were going through.'*

Such immense traumas and tragedies certainly leave mental scars for life. Because human's minds have their own pain threshold, once the agony goes above that edge, some people's minds can no longer take it and subsequently shut down: become non-responsive towards the outside world. Therefore it is not uncommon to see many insane people in the tsunami-hit area especially those who lost most of their family members and are left to fend the world alone. As for those, whose minds are not shut down, will have to bear excruciating mental pain. Having known how the mind works, these tsunami victims must feel as if 10 or 100 knives repeatedly stabbing into their hearts in every breath of every moment of their lives from now on.

Normality has disappeared from their lives: to some people for good. Unlike physical wound soon healed, this type of mental wound will not easily go away like the giant wave. It will stay for as long as it takes unless they know how to restore their normal minds and salvage normality back to their lives again. Indeed, the very least we can do is to pledge fund to help these people, our fellow human friends, to get back on their feet again so that they can rebuild their livelihoods.

It could be 'us!'

One thing for sure is that even though we are not the direct victims of this killer wave, neither did we lose our loved ones, we are still very much part of this tsunami casualties. This devastation has forced all of us to come to term with the cruel fact and the reality of life: we are mortal and we don't know what is just round the corner. We can't help thinking that this could happen to anyone of us, at anywhere and any time. It could be we who excitedly pack our bags, and catch a flight to go to the spot where we might die! Who knows? As life is an on-going process, how do we know sudden accidental death - either caused by man or nature - will not happen to us? We have no way to know, do we?

Blaming who?

When unfortunate and fatal events happen in our lives, it is natural that we want to blame someone (or something) who is responsible for our loss and pains. Retaliation and revenge, although morally wrong, can certainly smooth over a few rough edges of our mental wound. This very reason is definitely one of the main causes of most violence, destructions and particularly wars.

Nonetheless, what or whom exactly can we truly blame for these overwhelming pains inflicting on a mass number of humanity like this tsunami disaster? We, human, cannot be accounted for this ruthless onslaught of humanity, can we? The earthquake of 9.1 on the Richter scale, causing the earth to wobble and the snapping of the two tectonic plates, causing an explosion at the earth's core equivalent to 9,500 Hiroshima A-bombs, which sparked off this deadly tsunami on the Boxing Day morning of 2004, has nothing to do with man and global warming as the Green Campaigners would have wanted it to be. This, indeed, makes it even more difficult for us to deal with our raw and agonizing emotions because we have absolutely no one to be accounted for and to put the blame on as far as this enormity of human tragedy is concerned.

It maybe true that had we have the tsunami warning system in the Indian Ocean, many thousands of lives could have been saved like those in Thailand, India, Sri Lanka, the Maldives and Somalia. But this is it: as I said 'life is an on-going process and we don't have a clue what is round the corner.' Before we can learn from our mistakes, a high price must, unfortunately, be paid for the first lesson - shockingly high it is for the lesson of this Asian tsunami! Should we be able to predict our future, I don't know if it would make life easier or more difficult. I am afraid you have to be the judge of that.

Blaming Mother Nature?

If man, however, is not to be held responsible for this human catastrophe, what, then, left to be blamed is either Mother Nature or God: the meeting point between science and religion. We can say this is either the act of Nature or the act of God.

If this tsunami devastation was caused by the awesome act of nature, we cannot do anything about it but to accept, which is still not easy, as we all know. No matter how much and how precise geologists and all experts have explained to us about the cause of this huge earthquake in the Indian Ocean by Sumatra, we still find it extremely difficult to connect and comprehend how those rational information can make so many lives perish within a matter of minutes. It just doesn't make any sense in our heads, let alone in our hearts. At least it took Hitler, Mao and Pol Pot a length of time, years, to plan and to kill so many people, which make it easier to blame on those evil people. But with this Asian tsunami, it was a very short, sharp and swift ambush; no one can possibly prepare for this size of enormity all done and dusted within such a short time. Despite blaming this huge devastation on the act of nature, in the end, we still can't help feeling destroyed, outraged and asking: Why?

Blaming God!

If this, however, was the act of God, we have a much bigger 'WHY?' challenging us on our doorsteps. Why God want to play such a prank on his invention? Didn't 'HE' have better things to do - like catching and punishing the sinners roaming the world he built? Why did the God of love want to punish his own creation especially the children and the innocents who had committed no crime?

At least, Hitler had his reasons to kill young children: they had Jewish blood and would one day grow up into adult Jews. What, then, was the almighty God's reason to indiscriminately and mercilessly slaughter his children - his very own symbol of love, purity and innocence; the very group of human he most adores according to the Bible - in mass number?

The above poignant story of the Australian mother, who was forced to make an impossible and unthinkable choice as which son she should let go to die, sounded no difference from what the Nazis did to the Jews during the Holocaust and Pol Pot, to the Cambodians.

I heard some people believing that God was already dead at Auschwitz! Well, this depends entirely on how you define the word 'God', I suppose.

Nevertheless, the paralysing magnitude of this biblical catastrophe has undoubtedly raised a lot of challenging questions in people's minds, from the religious and non-religious alike. Even some clerics couldn't help but raise their eyebrows. The Christian faith unfortunately does not invite simplistic answers to the problem of human suffering, leaving people with lots of hung-up feelings: lost, outraged, confused, anguish and isolation. It doesn't matter what beliefs we have, we can't seem to get pass the simple question: WHY?

It's high time to reflect life!

Despite realizing the fact that some people do have short and selective memories, I hope that this Asian tsunami has, however, created the right atmosphere for some people - like you who are reading this very sentence - to reflect life and desperately want to find its true meaning and the real purpose of living.

As I am writing this paragraph, it is exactly 30 days after the deadly tsunami hit Asia. The mental wounds are still very raw especially those who are directly affected. It isn't difficult to understand that the only thing people want most right now is to return some normality back to their lives. But what specifically is normality? What precisely is the nature of a normal mind?

Summary

To answer this vital question, we must, first of all, identify the nature of the ultimate truth. This ultimate nature is the beginning (or/and the end) of this entangled ball of string. Once we can get hold of it, all the knots along the line can easily be straight out accordingly. This is the turning point where my entire work might be able to help you should you want to know the answer, of course.

Einstein Questions,
Buddha Answers

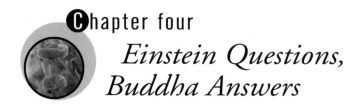

Chapter four
Einstein Questions, Buddha Answers

Albert Einstein's historic success happened 100 years ago. In 1905, he published 5 papers, one of which was the Theory of Relativity. As part of the celebration, there have been regular documentaries about Albert Einstein, some of which I watched while I've been writing this little book. This viewing has given me the insight and helped me tremendously to piece together all these following information and thoughts, which enable me to find the connection between the notions of Einstein and the Buddha.

The run-up to the Theory of Relativity

I feel most grateful to Albert Einstein, the Nobel Prize physicist, who posted the most vital question on behalf of humanity: what is the absolute ruling point in nature? He asked.

I am no scientist and don't have much clue what Einstein's general Theory of Relativity and the Quantum Mechanic are all about. I am only interested in why he needed to find the absolute ruling point in nature at the first place. From what I can gather, this absolute ruling point could be used as the fixed standard to measure everything against so that the result would be universally precise and accurate.

Einstein, however, failed to find such a definite ruling point because he found out that there is absolutely nothing standing still as the Universe is constantly moving, therefore everything is moving relatively. Consequently, we can only measure everything in a relative manner by nominating an assumed point, i.e.

our body weight is related to gravity, whatever our body weight is on earth, it will be less should we weigh ourselves on the moon since the moon has less gravity than earth. This initial notion is, nonetheless, the run-up to the Theory of Relativity - which is totally out of my range from then on! I hope I managed to get this primary notion of the world genius right though!

Put your hand on a hot stove for a minute, and it seems like an hour. Sit with a pretty girl for an hour, and it seems like a minute. THAT'S relativity, said Einstein.

Einstein's quest for the Theory of Everything

After the Theory of Relativity and his landmark discovery about the close link between energy and mass, $e = mc^2$ - the equation leading to the make of the lethal weapon, the nuclear bomb[7] - Einstein developed his Quantum Mechanic: finding out that everything in the universe working in the same way as throwing a dice. The result is based on probability, which is the very nature that Einstein could not surrender to.

---

[7]Einstein was a pacifist; he never thought that $e = mc^2$ would be developed into a nuclear bomb some 40 years after. Following his landmark discovery - that tiny amount of mass could be turned into immense energy should that mass be travelling at the speed of light square - Einstein gave interview to the media saying that to make that theory work, it could be comparing to shooting a bird in the dark in the country where there was not many birds around. He never thought that there would be any technology that could make this theory worked. However, one of his physicist friends worked out how to do it - by using the neutron to split the nucleus of the atom - its chain reactions could cause the immense energy, which could easily be developed into a nuclear bomb. This friend came to see Einstein in the US and asked him to write a letter to President Roosevelt because they were afraid that the Nazis would develop this nuclear technology used against the Allies in the war. What was supposed to be a warning letter to the President had given the United State the know-how technology of a nuclear bomb. The first ever nuclear bomb was finally made, deployed and dropped in Hiroshima in 1945, following with the second one in Nagasaki. Albert Einstein was devastated.

Basically he could not bear standing on lose ground (probability); what he needed was the solid base, where he thought only mathematics can offer. As a result, Einstein was downright hostile towards his own Quantum Mechanic and its performance despite the huge development. Einstein's Quantum Mechanic was the early stepping-stone leading to modern science and the subsequent technological advance of our modern time.

What held Einstein back was his religious nature, his belief in God. Together with his overwhelming passion in wanting to know the sheer precision of everything through mathematics, these two ingredients combined and triggered the chain reaction in the mind of the genius once again. Einstein endeavoured into a quest that constantly fed his mental hunger till the last moment of his life. He relentlessly tried to find a unified theory which, in his belief, would be able to give answer to everything and this result in his quest for The Theory of Everything - the persistent task that led the great man to his doom as the Theory of Everything never stood a chance in the scientific world.

God would not play dice

Einstein believed that the precise mathematics was the answer to everything and this too must be able to explain how God build the universe. As he said:

I want to know how God created this world. I am not interested in this or that phenomenon, in the spectrum of this or that element. I want to know His thoughts; the rest are details.

The Theory of Everything is his wanting to find an equation that can read the mind of God and his artwork in creating the universe. Although the nurse, tending at his dead bed, tried to tell him: *'maybe God didn't want us to know his mind,'* Einstein wouldn't have it. *'God would not play dice,'* said Einstein stubbornly. His quest was fruitless; he left the world without finding the answer.

Had he found it, the survivals of the holocaust, the Asian tsunami victims along with the rest of humanity, might be able to answer their challenging question beginning with the really big 'WHY?' Why did the almighty God not help his off springs at the most critical and most desperate moment of their lives?

Einstein's admission to Buddhism

Although Einstein left the world without finding the answer he had been looking for all his life, he, however, left the most valuable speech for mankind, for which I am immensely grateful. His following speech can still urge us to search further the fundamental questions he posted on behalf of humanity. Towards the end of his life while he was struggling to find the unified theory, he began to suspect that Buddhism might have the answer he was looking for. His book titled *'The Human Side'* published in 1954, Einstein said:

The religion of the future will be a cosmic religion. It should transcend a personal God and avoid dogmas and theology. Covering both natural and spiritual, it should be based on a religious sense arising from the experience of all things, natural and spiritual and a meaningful unity. Buddhism answers this description. If there is any religion that would cope with modern scientific needs, it would be Buddhism.[8]

The great man was spot on. The unified theory for everything that Einstein was looking for, had been answered by the Buddha over two thousands five hundred years earlier.

Einstein questions, Buddha answers

As far as I am concerned, Einstein's initial notion of wanting to find the absolute ruling point and his quest for the unified theory refered to the same wish. Fundamentally, the world genius wanted to find something that was absolute, solid, definite, ever-lasting and

---

[8]Albert Einstein, 1954, from Albert Einstein: The Human Side, edited by Helen Dukas and Banesh Hoffman, Princeton University Press.

unchanged so that he could eternally and unconditionally rely on this very final certainty. These definite descriptions also sound very much like the nature of God or eternity, don't they?

It is beyond any doubt that the final ruling point and the unfound unified theory cannot be anything else but the nature of the absolute truth or Nirvana in Buddhist terminology.

Mankind must know that this ultimate nature does exist. The Buddha found it on the night of his enlightenment exactly 2593 years ago. Indeed, all through the history of Buddhism, there have always been some enlightened followers who came forward and confirmed the nature of the ultimate truth or Nirvana, which is one of the main reasons that keep Buddhism and its culture alive till today. The ultimate truth will certainly perform the same nature and giving the same result at absolutely every time and place in the entire universe. This definite reliable nature is exactly what Albert Einstein had been looking for all along.

The truth is right in front of our nose!

Following my 'Eureka experience!' I can now confidently share with you that the answer to the absolute ruling point in nature and the unified theory has been, all along, hidden in the legendary perception of the two trains running at the same speed. Despite having seen the truth himself, Einstein could not work the answer out because his brain was too busy thinking: *what on earth had two in a week and one in a year?!*

Indeed, the ultimate truth cannot be found by the power of human brain; it must be initially pointed out by those who themselves have been through the ultimate enlightenment. To tackle the ultimate truth is based on the principle of sheer common sense and simplicity, which make it extremely difficult for us to understand, especially intellectual genius, who are keen to delve into their tubes of intellect.

Here and Now[9]

'Here and now' is the exact answer the great man would have wanted to locate but failed; it is hidden in between the two trains running at the same speed. 'Here and now' is, indeed, the absolute ruling point in nature. This chapter will help you to understand the preliminary concept of 'here and now' as the nature of the truth, simplicity and normality.

However, trying to have access to 'here and now' is indeed another matter. It involves practising certain mental skill: very much like learning how to balance a surfing board up and down the different sizes of waves.

Human mind is a funny old thing!

All professional writers know that they should face mental block when they begin their piece of work with a wrong sentence or wrong paragraph. Although

---

[9]Chapter two 'Here and Now' my book titled *Do You Know What A Normal Mind Is?*

it may sound beautiful and seem perfect, writers can't move on unless they try other sentence, maybe with different approach. The change of the sentence and approach may sound a bit dowdy, not attractive but it works wonder as it takes away the obstacle and allow the brain (the mind) to work - flowing like tab water!

Human mind is a funny old thing. You must know how to handle the mind skilfully to make it work well for you. If not, you get nowhere. It works the same when we piece jigsaw puzzle together. Unskilful people will begin piecing the jigsaw puzzles without grouping the pieces first, which would make them progress very slowly. Whereas skilful player will group the different colours of the pieces and will certainly begin from the straight edges; with this strategy, they will progress much quicker.

The parable above was what happened to Albert Einstein including all academic thinkers (apart from those with vipassana skill). 'The position A' I talked about in 'The Final Frontier' is, in fact, the very nature of here and now: the nature of the ultimate truth or the absolute ruling point in nature. They all refer to the same ultimate nature and it is already right here in front of our nose! My students know this ultimate experience as 'the innocent perception.'

Without this realisation, due to the lack of enlightening guidance, ignorant people would naturally abandon the position A (the ultimate truth) and quickly enter 'the tube of intellect': the moment of posting the wrong question, wrong approach and wrong introduction, which causes the subsequent mental block.[10]

Intellect: our doomed vessel!

Our tube of intellect is indeed the very nature of our mental block in a much sinister and cunning character, yet, fundamentally profound. Intellect or the whole of our thinking faculty is man's fundamental tool used for acquiring knowledge and resulting in our civilisation. Should I compare our intellect as a vessel,

---

[10]Chapter four and five 'The Final Frontier' and 'The Tube of Intellect' my book titled *Do You Know What A Normal Mind Is?*

at the bottom of this vessel has an undetected hole. This vessel cannot go very far; sooner or later, it will sink!

Having been used as the fundamental tool and having no other tool left to rectify itself, the illusive quality of our intellect tricks us to believe that our mental proliferation is of positive nature. We must not be fooled by our technological development because at the end of our tube of intellect is nothing more than a cul-de-sac! We must admit that the advances of science along with our high-tech culture have offered us far more than we really need to live a life. Still, we are not content and happy, are we? Why? Ask...we must!

The way that Einstein explore into his mathematics, trying to come up with a unified theory was nothing more than his abandonment of position A - deserting the truth or the absolute ruling point he passionately wanted to find at the first place - and eagerly entering the tube of intellect. His mental pursuit is the equivalent to starting the wrong sentence or being an unskilful jigsaw puzzle player. As he walked deeper into his tube of intellect towards the 10th inch mark, a dead end was all he found.

The relative nature is the same as suffering

The relative nature of everything certainly extends to our mental state too. It can be allegorised as our mental nature standing on lose shaky ground. This unstable predicament is the nature of suffering or impermanence in the Buddha's term. This shaky relative nature (suffering) had urged the young prince Sidhardha to find the end of suffering and Einstein to pursue his quest for the Theory of Everything: the mind of God. Indeed, the Buddha found it but unfortunately, not Albert Einstein.

Without this fundamental wisdom pinning on to my backbone, I cannot possibly confirm to you that the ultimate truth is not at all remote - absolutely not in the space or to be found out after we die! It is right here in front of our nose all the time. *If the truth is not right here in front of us, where do we think we can find it?*

It doesn't matter what political and religious beliefs you have, there is only ONE ultimate truth. You can disagree or argue till your face turn blue, it doesn't change the fact that there is only ONE ultimate truth.

We fail to spot it because we don't have the right tool for the right job. The ultimate truth is waiting right here for everyone to uncover, it is not reserved only for monks, priests and spiritual people. It is absolutely for all of us regardless of age, genders, races, nations and beliefs. Should we have the right tool for the right job, we can uncover the ultimate truth all the same. This is a guarantee.

Vipassana

What so special about the Buddha is that following his discovery of the ultimate knowledge, he had also given us 'the distinctive way' so that his followers can reach this ultimate nature just like he did.

The Buddhist practice of the four foundations of mindfulness or vipassana is the tool leading us to have access to the ultimate truth. This practice can be easily adapted and performed within any religious environment as well as making it as a neutral exercise like what I do in my Tai chi class. Vipassana is nothing more than a mental skill as learning to observe our breathing, movements and sensations including our inner phenomena created by our thoughts, memories and feelings. It is a very scientific means suitable for all beliefs, religious and non-religious.

Vipassana can give us back our 6th sense, the very sense that every single human being has all the same. Man is the being with six senses and not five, this is the most important piece of information humanity must know. Our 6th sense is the ultimate tool we need should we want to rectify the fault of our intellect - our doomed vessel!

Losing the use of sight is a huge loss for an individual, we are now talking about mankind lose the use of our 6th sense all the same. Our global education is based on the understanding that human has five senses and, therefore, our education is defective from the start.

This is the main reason that causes all the entangled knots in my allegorical ball of cotton and why humanity cannot live in harmony despite all the efforts we have put in to secure world peace.

Among all the evil elements, ignorance, the Buddha says, is the worst. I hope you realise the enormity of this human catastrophe as far as the ignorance towards our 6th sense is concerned.

Vipassana is the formula for world peace

It is a shame that Albert Einstein didn't have a chance to bump into a vipassana teacher during his time, otherwise the world might be much different from what it is now. With the zeal from the great man like Einstein, it could well mean that vipassana might have been globally recognised as a strict scientific means to restore mental stability and normality. This first class recognition would subsequently have guided the scientific research about 'human's mind' towards the right direction: taking the blindfold off the 6th sense instead of tighten it up. The right research on mind issue would consequently have saved humanity from the 'drug culture', in which we are badly trapped today. This may be bad news for those who make billions from the drugs industry but it certainly is good news for humanity.

With the green light from the Nobel peace prize physicists like Einstein, vipassana could have well become the main component of our mainstream education across the globe. Vipassana is the first domino that will collapse all nature of problems surfacing from the heart of an individual human being all the way to the whole of humankind. This is the only formula for world peace and it is indeed what Einstein would have wanted to see, as he was very much a peace lover.

If A equals success, then the formula is: A=X+Y+Z. X is work. Y is play. Z is keep your mouth shut, said Einstein without knowing vipassana.

Had Einstein known vipassana, he might have said this instead:

If A equals world peace, then the formula is A=X+Y+Z. X is inner peace in all men, Y is inner peace in all women, Z is keep our mouths shut.

Moral relativism

Due to the lack of true wisdom, The Theory of Relativity has influenced our contemporary way of thinking leading to moral relativism. Because we think that there is no moral absolute - which there isn't - therefore, we judge our actions whether good or bad, moral or immoral, in a relative manner. Consequently, common thieves are allowed to class themselves better persons than first time murderers who feel better persons still than serial killers. This relative way of thinking can go on forever in both directions: good and bad.

Moral relativism, consequently, is responsible for the dramatic decline of morality throughout the world community because we can always find someone morally worse to level with, which make us feel a bit better about ourselves. Because the world is engulfed by so many problems and immoral people is unfortunately on the increase. With the inclination of using corrupted people as the assumed standard, immoral conducts flourish and become more acceptable. Infidelity, used to be morally wrong, become more common because it has been practised among the rich and the famous - some government ministers, some prime minister, some president, teachers, even monks and clerics! The breaking up of family units and poor parenting leave fewer people become qualified to be role models for our young generation. All these result in a massive moral vacuum. Consequently, morality is brought down to its knee, ensuing in more chaos and endless entangled social problems.

The ultimate ruling point can eliminate moral relativism

To eliminate our confusing social and moral climate, we must stop moral relativism. To do that, we must know the reason behind classical moral guidelines; society must know why every saint in the past gave us the same message telling us to be morally good. The ultimate ruling point or the ultimate truth is the only entity that can straight out all these moral and social confusion humanity is facing. There are, in fact, very good reasons behind moral conducts.

This brings us back to Einstein's initial notion again why we need to know the absolute ruling point in nature. Should we find that ultimate ruling point, society will have a chance to restore order and bring back true normality - although such a chance seems remote, we should at least try our very best first. The difference between having and not having the ultimate ruling point is extremely dramatic and irreplaceable. Without the fixed point to measure against, everything is freely shifting, letting lose and subjective, which finally result in the unhelpful moral relativism. Whereas with the definite ruling point, the result will be absolute, no longer subject to individual interpretation. We would consequently know exactly why we have to be morally good. I have talked about this issue quite extensively in *A Handful of Leaves* and *The User Guide to Life.*

Why genius prefer simple jobs

Some years ago, I watched a documentary following up the lives of a few adults whose IQ were exceedingly high since very young age and were labelled 'children prodigies.' While the world expected to see these whiz kids holding prominent academic careers in their adulthoods, they, instead, turned out to be a plumber, a carpenter, a farmer or a chef.

My allegorical tube of intellect can clearly explain why. It is because masterminds know it as a fact that one door is merely opened to yet another door and another endlessly, there is no exit (solution) as far as the use of the brain is concerned. Once intellectual geniuses have reached the brick wall of the 10th inch mark in the tube of intellect, it is a natural process that they would make a U-turn and find their way back to position A (the innocent world). Through experience, they will soon find out that the simplicity and ordinariness surrounding every avenue of their lives have much better tastes than exercising the power of their brains. It takes a genius to understand a genius. This is the reason why those whiz kids ended up doing simple jobs instead of joining the glory of the intellectual world.

Making a U-turn

Albert Einstein was one among those geniuses who was in the process of making a U-turn and heading towards position A as his speeches contained the high level of simplicity, normality and ordinariness: the outstanding quality of the truth or the innocent world. These following quotes by Einstein I located from a website are the clear signs of his enthusiasm supporting the fact that he was engaging in his outward-bound journey towards the 1st inch mark. They are:

1. *A table, a chair, a bowl of fruit and a violin; what else does a man need to be happy.*
2. *Gravitation cannot be held responsible for people falling in love.*
3. *Try not to become a man of success but rather to become a man of value.*
4. *We should take care not to make the intellect our god; it has, of course, powerful muscles, but no personality.*

5. *The whole of science is nothing more than a refinement of everyday thinking.*
6. *Problems cannot be solved at the same level of awareness that created them.*
7. *The only source of knowledge is experience.*
8. *If I had my life to live over again, I'd be a plumber.*
9. *All our lauded technological progress - our very civilization - is like the axe in the hand of the pathological criminal.*

Summary

Although Einstein left the world without knowing the ultimate truth, his legacy stays especially the fundamental questions he posted on behalf of humanity and his pointing towards Buddhism. His notions can certainly raise the awareness about the wisdom of the Buddha and bridge the gap between science and religion: bringing the believers and non-believers meeting at the central stage of the truth, honesty and humility.

This is the very aim that I have been trying my best to do - presenting the truth to you in a neutral approach, away from the framework of conflicting religions. I hope my work has done justice to both the Buddha and Albert Einstein.

Einstein Questions, Buddha Answers
Please Help Me To Help Others

Birmingham, UK
17 February 2004
Dear all,

Many years ago when I was struggling to get *A Handful of Leaves* published in the UK, I wrote a letter to The Reverend Desmond Tutu, the Bishop of Cape Town. I thought that if he could agree with what I said in this book and could write a foreword for me, it would be a great opportunity to introduce the four foundations of awareness (vipassana) to the Christians as I have no doubt that vipassana is for humanity and definitely not just for the Buddhists. At that time, although the content of that book was about taking care of an individual human as well as the world community, I felt totally alone. I couldn't help thinking that I must be totally mad sitting here, writing all these challenging words without any support from anyone since no one knew what I was doing at the time. My determination was so strong that I quoted a couple sentences from the film *Titanic*, which had just been released at the time. The part when Jack was locked up in a room and Rose was trying frantically to find him as the ship was sinking. She bumped into the ship architect so she forcefully asked him where that room was. Rose looked at him in the eyes and said: *"I will find him, with or without your help but with your help, I would do better."* These two sentences stayed with me; I always remember them because it was my character.

In the letter to the Reverend of Cape Town, I felt that it was necessary for him to have some idea about my true character because I was an unknown person and he didn't know me personally. After I talked about the purpose of my work, I told him that I was determined to carry my work through with or without his help but with his help, I would do better.

Indeed, I caught the Reverend's attention; he kindly wrote back to me and admired my compassionate intention. He also apologised that he could not possibly write the preface for my book because of his tight schedule, his workloads as well as his weak health. He did, however encourage me to persevere with my charitable work and wished me all the best of luck and success. I was so happy to receive his letter and whole-heartedly understood his reasons. His encouragement was enough to inspire me to work hard until today.

As you know, Dr. Thongchai Rojkangsadan, a lecturer of the Computer Engineering Department of Chulalongkorn University, Bangkok, Thailand, is working on a website for me. I would like to have a file containing feedback from my students and readers. Like most people, whenever I buy a book, I go straight to the back cover and read the blurb and also the short critiques. Although we know that the author would never think about putting negative criticism at the back of one's own book, positive critiques still influence the readers to buy the book. I intend to put my three books in the website so that people can help themselves. My point is that I am still a very anonymous person. Being a woman without any support from the establishments such as religion and education, I can do very little comparing to the huge message I want to deliver to humanity. Therefore, with the very limited resources I have, I intend to use them to the full potential. Your feedback will be one of the significant resources I can use. To make this website more effective, potential readers need to be convinced whether it would be worth their time to browse through my website or not. This is where your help will be very much appreciated. To help you have the perspective regarding my work, I will summarise the whole structure of my written work and teaching in class.

The goal of my work is to tell humanity that:

1) The "ultimate truth" does exist.

2) Saints in the past have called the ultimate nature Nirvana, God, The Tree of Life or Tao. My role is to simplify the holy words and unite them by leading people to witness a simple experience called the "innocent perception."

3) The four foundations of awareness or vipassana is the method leading people to the ultimate

truth or the innocent perception and to encourage as many people as possible to take part in the vipassana practice.

4) Tai chi and Qi gong movements can be the ideal non-religious ways helping people to witness the ultimate truth.

I would be so grateful if you could help me to help others by writing a few sentences telling others how you had benefited from my works. You are welcome to bring up one issue that you feel compelled to talk about and how my work had helped you to understand - if not, just general feedback. Please state your name as well as your profession and credentials as these things are still important to potential readers. Please kindly email your feedback to me so I can compile them into a file for Khun Thongchai to transfer onto the website.

My students who know me personally know how determined I am. As I said to the Reverend Desmond Tutu, I would deliver the above messages to my fellow human beings with or without your help but with your help, I could do better. I don't mean to be harsh or threatening, I am just in the mood to use this line since it fits into the right context, that's all. Many thanks in advance.

I hope you are still working hard with your practice. Please persevere despite any obstacles you may encounter.

With metta,
Supawan

Einstein Questions, Buddha Answers
How Can You Help Supawan?

I hope you enjoyed reading this book. Should you agree with me and would like to take part in helping me spread the words of truth to humankind, here are a few things you are able to do:

1) Introducing my books or website to at least one person whom you care most or who are right and ready to listen to my message.

2) Donating my books to at least one library.

3) Pledge towards my printing fund, which is used to print both my Thai and English titles. There is a long list of books waiting to be published and made accessible for wider audiences especially my English books, which unfortunately are only on sale in Thailand. I lack the human resources to help me take my books to English speaking countries. The price of the books, especially the Thai titles, are intentionally marked lower

than usual to make them affordable for all, therefore the profit made from the sale is on the minimum. Your pledge will certainly be well spent to propagate the truth. Please kindly transfer funds to the following bank account.

Name of account: Khun Patarachai Amorntham Bangkok Bank, Chan Road, Sapan 5, Savings account no. 219-0-38434-3

4) Please pledge towards this one-off fund to aid the travelling expenses for my Cameroonian students to join the retreat in Thailand in July 2005 as a way to spread the seedling of the truth to Africa. (Chapter 10: Please help Africa with me! Book titled Do You Know What A Normal Mind Is?) To ensure I have sufficient funds for this purpose, the profit made from the sale of this book will be put towards this project. Therefore the sale price may be slightly higher than usual. The Cameroon fund account is:

Name of account: Khun Patarachai Amorntham Bangkok Bank, Chan Road, Sapan 5, Savings account no. 219-0-39747-7

Following your money transfer, please kindly email:

Khun Patarachai <u>pamornt@ji-net.com</u> and

Khun Thongchai <u>thongnet@yahoo.com</u>

Alternatively, you may phone Khun Patarachai to confirm your money transfer 00-66- 0-1300-4624

When I was a little girl, I often told myself that one day should I become rich, I would use my wealth to help the poor and ease their suffering. To fulfil my childhood dream, should this printing fund be healthy in the far future, a regular fixed percentage will be donated to fund other charitable tasks: creating jobs for my students in Cameroon or other places, donating directly to other charities to help the poor and the needy, the list goes on. This is my desire that will be discussed and done when the time is right, even if it means after I die.

I would like to take this opportunity to thank you in advance for your help in whatever way you choose from the above.

Supawan Green
Birmingham
11 February 2005

Details Of The Retreat In July 2005

The first step of any journey, not to mention the spiritual journey, is known to be difficult. Spending three days with me is aimed to help you to take that very first step of this long-haul journey to the ultimate truth. This is the part that I cannot teach you by writing alone: it has to be a direct teaching.

With the aid of my toy box, I will show you how the five elements, which constitute human life form, body and mind, works. You will learn the following:

1) Locating the nature of your 6th sense (or your 'mental self'). This is a crucial stage, without your fundamental tool, you won't be able to take that vital first step. In the case that you may have been practising vipassana for a number of years, but feel that you haven't yet progressed to a level of your satisfaction, it could mean that you haven't yet properly located the nature of

your 6th sense. You may have been using your 6th sense in an obscure manner, which results in the restriction of the use of your mind's eye. By joining the retreat, your 6th sense will be properly underlined; consequently you will be able to excel in your journey.

2) Learning the skill of bringing your mental self back to your four homes: the four foundations of mindfulness. You will be taught to develop your meditation skills through your daily activities, as your four homes are literally there already!

3) Getting to know your inner battlefield between Tom and Jerry and how to keep Jerry at bay.

4) Understanding the nature of our mental hologram and how to tackle the most difficult nature in the universe: mental illusion!

5) Getting to know the face of your 4th home: the innocent perception. Not knowing the nature of the truth or the innocent perception, is yet another factor that delays your spiritual journey towards your ultimate enlightenment. Once you have glimpsed the innocent

perception, the four foundations of mindfulness has completed its full cycle. You will then be able to spend the rest of your life training your mental self to return to your four homes.

The mental skills will leave you spiritually wealthy. You don't have to read yet another book, if you don't want to. This practice will, however, allow you to live your life to the full and be able to carry you through until you have your very own 'Eureka experience!'

Should you want to join this retreat in Thailand on the 18th-20th July 2005, please secure your place by emailing Khun Thongchai: thongnet@yahoo.com

Please enrol as soon as you can, as there is a lot of organising involved. Should the number of participants exceed the quota, an additional retreat may be set up. The cost for the retreat will be based on your kind contributions towards the cost of food and venue, which has yet to be decided at this stage. It is likely to take place somewhere in Bangkok. The details will be posted on my website www.supawangreen.in.th soon.

Ⓔinstein Questions, Ⓑuddha Answers

Works By Supawan Green

English Titles:

Dear Colin: What is the Meaning of Life? Minerva Press (liquidated)

Can a Caterpillar be Perfect? Mental Health Publication, Thailand

A Handful of Leaves Mental Health Publication

The User Guide to Life Mental Health Publication

Do You Know What A Normal Mind Is? Skybook

Einstein Questions, Buddha Answers Skybook

Thai Titles:

ใบไม้กำมือเดียว สำนักพิมพ์สุขภาพใจ

คู่มือชีวิต ภาคศีลธรรม สำนักพิมพ์สกายบุ๊กส์

คู่มือชีวิต ภาคกฎแห่งกรรม สำนักพิมพ์สกายบุ๊กส์

อวดอุตริมนุสธรรมที่มีในตน สำนักพิมพ์สกายบุ๊กส์

For more information, please email Supawan@ blueyonder.co.uk or visit my website www.supawangreen.in.th or write to:

Supawan Green

Tai chi and Meditation

The Munrow Sport Centre

The University of Birmingham

Bristol Road South

Edgebaston

Birmingham, B15 2TT

Great Britain

New Release

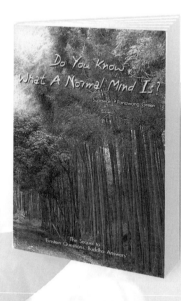

Do You Know
What A Normal Mind Is?
Pages No. 256
price 250 Baht

This book is about Buddhism in a non-religious or scientific approach. The main purpose of this book is about guiding the right direction to life. This book also talks about the direction to find the ultimate truth and finding out what "the normal mind" is. It also talks about guiding people to distinguish the intellectual knowledge from the spiritual knowledge like Buddhism.

Distributed by :
Skybook Company Limited
Tel :   (662) 958-1125-7
            (662) 567-5119
Fax :   (662) 567-5105
e-mail: sales@skybook.co.th
www.skybook.co.th